sophy

tor

elaware)

g/Bowling Green State

y)

)

ty)

ty of New York at Albany)

ity University of New York)

versity, New Orleans)

University)

Frontiers of Philo

Peter H. Hare, Series Edi

Advisory Board

Norman E. Bowie (University of D

Antony Flew (University of Readin
University)

Jesse Kalin (Vassar College)

E. D. Klemke (Iowa State Universit

Alice Lazerowitz (Smith College)

Morris Lazerowitz (Smith College

Joseph Margolis (Temple Universi

Robert G. Meyers (State Universi

Gerald Myers (Graduate Center, C

Sandra B. Rosenthal (Loyola Uni

T. L. Short (Kenyon College)

Richard A. Watson (Washington

LATIN AMERICAN PHILOSOPHY

IN THE TWENTIETH CENTURY

MAN, VALUES, AND

THE SEARCH FOR

PHILOSOPHICAL

IDENTITY

EDITED BY JORGE J. E. GRACIA

With translations by William Cooper, Francis M. Myers,
Iván Jaksić, Donald L. Schmidt, Charles Schofield, and Jorge J. E. Gracia

PROMETHEUS BOOKS
700 East Amherst St., Buffalo, New York 14215

Risieri Frondizi and Francis M. Myers,
in memoriam

Published 1986 by Prometheus Books
700 East Amherst Street, Buffalo, New York 14215
Copyright © 1986 by Jorge J. E. Gracia
All Rights Reserved

Library of Congress Cataloging-in-Publication Data

Latin American philosophy in the twentieth century.

(Frontiers of philosophy)
1. Philosophy. 2. Philosophy, Latin American.
I. Gracia, Jorge J. E. II. Series.
B29.L295 1986   199'.8   86-91551
ISBN 0-87975-333-1

Contents

6   Contents

PART THREE: THE SEARCH FOR PHILOSOPHICAL IDENTITY

Preface

A collection of philosophical readings is justified if it responds to a need. Its quality, however, depends on the authors and texts that it includes and on the help it may provide for better understanding the issues on which the collection is built.

That the English-speaking world needs a representative collection of readings from Latin American philosophers is beyond dispute: only two such collections exist. The first one, entitled *Contemporary Latin American Philosophy* (1954), is a translation of an anthology originally published by Aníbal Sánchez Reulet in 1949. Apart from the fact that the book has been out of print for almost thirty years, it should be clear from its year of publication that it is dated. The other collection is my recently published *Philosophical Analysis in Latin America* (1984), but this is a specialized text that deals only with the impact of the analytic movement in Latin America. Given the growing importance of Latin America in the world today, some account must be taken of the philosophic thought of the area. American scholars have already taken note of the so-called "boom" of the Latin American novel and of the flowering of other forms of literature, but they have for the most part neglected the development of philosophical thought in the region.

The preparation of a truly representative collection of readings from Latin American philosophers presents serious difficulties. Generally, Latin American thinkers have an extensive list of publications. In several cases, their collected works extend to more than twenty volumes. Other difficulties are the heterogeneity of the themes in their works, and the uneven quality of the writings. These characteristics stem largely from the variety of responsibilities these authors have assumed and the demands of the activities in which they have engaged. Furthermore, part of their writings is scattered in short-lived journals that are difficult to locate. The abundance, diversity, and difficult access of the material are bewildering to one who does not know where to begin. Perhaps this explains why Latin American authors are more often mentioned than read, and why we lack a representative collection of readings in English.

9

The present collection has been gathered from the works of only major Latin American thinkers and is meant as a guide in the study of their thought. It aims to be a point of departure rather than an end, encouraging careful study of the works from which the texts are taken, and supporting the efforts of those who wish to continue the study of its basic themes.

The selections included here are limited to twentieth-century authors. Such a restriction could be justified as conventional procedure, but there is a more important reason for it: the preceding centuries provide few authentic philosophical works. Indeed, pressured by more urgent needs, Latin America did not often confront the study of philosophy for its own sake until the beginning of this century.

In order to avoid a general and disconnected work, the collection has been focused on three fundamental and concrete problems, thereby maintaining a certain unity. This approach has the added advantage of making it possible to retain a general perspective while avoiding the risk of superficiality. The three themes in question were chosen not only because of the special attention they have received from Latin American thinkers, but also because these issues—the interpretations of man and value and the search for philosophical identity—often lay bare the root and intellectual orientation of Latin American culture. Owing to these thematic limitations, several thinkers of significant stature, such as Mariátegui, Ardao, Larroyo, and others, have been omitted, but this shortcoming seemed small if compared with the advantages of following the chosen procedure.

The authors' importance has been one of the fundamental basis for their inclusion. This importance was measured by the theoretical quality of their ideas and the influence they have had in Latin America. Space limitations, however, demanded the exclusion of many pages from each author, exclusions that were neither easy nor pleasant. The pages presented here were selected from thousands studied over a period of years. The choice, therefore, was neither hasty nor uninformed.

There were also other considerations that determined the inclusion of some authors and texts and the exclusion of others. For example, thinkers such as Octavio Paz, José Enrique Rodó, Jackson de Figuereido, and José Pereira de Graza Aranha were left out because of the purely philosophical nature of the collection and their more literary approach to ideas. None of the Spanish *trasterrados* (Xirau, Gaos, Nicol, García Bacca, Ferrater Mora, Recaséns Siches, and so many others) who have contributed so much to the development of philosophy in Latin America have been included. Members of the analytic movement, such as Carrió, Bunge, and Castañeda, have not been anthologized because their work is already known and available in the United States, either directly or through the collection of papers referred to earlier. Latin American Thomists like Derisi and Amoroso Lima have also been excluded because their philosophical position does not differ significantly from that of Thomists elsewhere. Finally, space restrictions have made it impossible to include selections from such important figures as Delgado, Vasallo, Pucciarelli, Rougés, Alberini, Llambías de Azevedo, García Maynez, Ferreira da Silva, Millas, Molina, Mayz Vallenilla, Schwartzmann, Dussel, and many others who have made important contributions to philosophical anthropology, axiology, and the issue of philosophical identity in Latin America.

This work is introduced by an essay on contemporary Latin American philosophy. Each of the three parts into which the book is divided is also introduced by an essay, the first on man, the second on value, and the third on the search for philosophical identity. Each essay summarizes the more prevalent approaches to its theme and introduces the thought of the philosophers whose writings have been included. A brief biographical sketch precedes each author's text. Added at the end is a select bibliography that is meant to provide helpful information and also to serve as a guide for future research; it should not be regarded as exhaustive.

The selections included in the first two parts were made in collaboration with Risieri Frondizi, who was the senior editor of a more extensive collection, published in Spanish and Portuguese, entitled *El hombre y los valores en la filosofía latinoamericana del siglo XX* (1975; reprint, México: Fondo de Cultura Económica, 1980). The introductory essays to those parts as well as the biographical sketches of the various authors contained therein have also been translated from that edition, although modifications were introduced in order to adapt them to the new context. The authors responsible for the introduction and sketches are identified at the end of each by their initials. The textual selections follow the order of the discussion in the introductory essays. Square brackets indicate additions made by the editor or the translators.

The institutions and persons who have provided assistance in the preparation of this work are numerous. To each of them I would like to express my profound appreciation, but limitations of space prevent me from doing so explicitly in every case. I am particularly grateful, however, to Mrs. Josefina Barbat de Frondizi for her permission to print Frondizi's introductory essays and for allowing me to edit them to fit the present context. I am also grateful to the translators of the texts, who spent long hours at their difficult task. It should be added here that William Cooper is responsible for all the translations, including those of the introductions and biographical sketches, except for those of the texts from Frondizi, Korn, Deústua, Reale, Zea, Roig, Bondy, the introduction to the third part, and the biographical sketches to Zea, Roig, and Bondy. The introduction and biographical sketches of the third part and the Frondizi selection in the first part were written in English by their respective authors. The texts from Korn and Deústua were translated by Francis Myers, the text from Zea by Iván

Jaksić, the text from Bondy by Donald L. Schmidt, the text from Roig by Charles Schofield, and the text from Reale by Jorge J. E. Gracia. Finally, I would also like to thank the authors and publishers who generously granted permission for the publication of the texts included here.

The Editor
1985

Introduction

Major trends in contemporary Latin American philosophy emerged from the reaction against positivism.

Excepting scholasticism, positivism is the most widespread and deeply rooted philosophical movement in Latin America. The depth of its impact was due to historical factors: it arrived at the proper time and it addressed the needs of that age. This positive philosophy, developed by the Frenchman Auguste Comte (1793–1857), attempted to develop a rigorous, systematic understanding of man both as an individual and as a social being. Comte sought to base his understanding on experience and reason and to let it serve as a means for solving social problems. To achieve this objective, he sought to impose upon the study of human affairs the methods, criteria of truth, and conceptual precision that had borne such excellent results in the natural sciences. He coined the term "sociology" to designate the new science of social phenomena and gave special attention to its development. He maintained that the sciences were characterized by an undeniable unity and could be arranged in hierarchical order, according to the degree of mathematization they would allow, with physics as the fundamental science and sociology the less scientific. Sociology, the newest and most complex of the sciences, required much empirical investigation before its discoveries could be reduced to mathematically formulated laws.

Comte was not moved by a mere desire to know. Knowledge was a servant of action and should lead to the solution of concrete problems. This practical aspect, perhaps, was one of the most captivating for Latin Americans, who desired to overcome anarchy, eradicate misery and disease, and place their own countries on the path of progress.

This, however, was not the only reason for the wide acceptance that positivism experienced. There were also reasons of a strictly cultural and theoretical nature. Latin America had been nurtured in scholasticism and consequently, the sciences of man were in a deplorable state. Conceptual and terminological vagueness, irresponsible speculation, as well as unfounded and archaic dogmatism were predominant characteristics. Positivism, however, brought principles based on experience and logical rigor, and offered

13

the assurance of constant progress, insisting that its claims rested on proved knowledge. There would be no more fruitless theories, idle speculations, and vain attempts. At last a sound procedure had been found that, although it required great effort, would lead to the gradual solution of Latin America's problems.

Furthermore, positivism benefited greatly from the prestige of science. It was then natural that scientific prestige should be transferred to positivism, since the latter proposed to limit its methods to those used by science. It was believed that a new era had begun in which scientific study would make it possible to find the causes of social evils and to eliminate them, just as medicine had begun to eradicate endemic diseases.

Comte's law of the three stages also captured the attention of many Latin Americans. This law claims that humanity passes through three stages, the theological, the metaphysical, and the scientific or positive. In the theological stage, the interpretation of reality is founded on prejudices and superstitions. The metaphysical stage is dominated by speculation in which facts are either ignored or are not given adequate attention. Finally, in the positive stage, speculation is replaced by the confirmation of facts and their rigorous interpretation, and knowledge is founded upon experience.

Latin American thinkers applied this law to the history of their own countries and believed the law was confirmed by experience. An example of this attitude is found in the *Civic Oration* that was delivered by the Mexican positivist Gabino Barreda in Guanajuato (1867), in which he refers to and applies the ideas of Comte. Having this oration in mind, President Benito Juárez named Barreda as a member of a committee to draft the law, approved on December 2, 1867, that gave birth to public education in Mexico. The fact that another great teacher, Justo Sierra, succeeded to Barreda's position and continued to apply positivist principles to educational policy, explains the strength that this perspective acquired and its predominance in Mexico until the fall of the dictator Porfirio Díaz in 1911. Positivism was the official philosophy during the twenty-seven years of the dictatorship of General Díaz, whose government was guided by Comte's slogan "Order and progress."

The chaos and backwardness that prevailed in some Latin American countries explain why positivist ideas captivated the minds of so many thinkers and politicians.

Positivism made a significant impact in Brazil, where the positivist slogan, "Order and progress," was incorporated into the Brazilian flag and into the attitude of its political leaders.

Positivism also exercised a strong influence on Argentine education, especially in the "School of Paraná," where Scalabrini, Ferreira, Herrera, and others provided leadership. This prestige was further enhanced by the tenaciousness of José Ingenieros and his works, by the *Revista de Filosofía,* and by the Cultura Argentina publishing house.

As is natural, positivism developed its own distinctive mode in each country. Ideas acquired new life in crossing the Atlantic, and they developed according to the sociocultural ecology of each country. One should also keep in mind that Latin American positivism was nurtured principally by two sources, Comte and Herbert Spencer (1820–1903). The latter, a proponent of evolutionism, was considered a positivist in Spanish America, as occurred also with John Stuart Mill. However, Comte and Spencer differed in their intellectual orientation, one being French and the other English, and the quality of the positivism in any given country was affected by the degree to which one or the other of these men exercised the predominant influence. Generally, the ideas of Comte had a greater weight in Brazil, Mexico, and Chile, whereas Spencer received greater attention in Argentina, Uruguay, and Cuba. On some occasions, due to political considerations, the influence within each country varied, as in the case of Cuba, where Enrique José Varona rejected Comte's ideas because they did not favor the emancipation of that country from Spanish rule and instead gave preference to Spencer and his idea of liberty.

In spite of these and many other national differences, one can speak of Latin American positivism as a unified, yet evolving trend in which the influence of Comte is greater toward the beginning, and that of Spencer predominates toward the end. John Stuart Mill's influence was a subsequent and minor development.

Due to the inflexibility of Comte's ideas, the reactionary attitude in the final period of his life when he founded the "religion of humanity," and his approval of the coup d'état of Napoleon III in 1851, Comte's thought was rejected more violently than was Spencer's.

The general decline of positivism stems from several factors. National distinctions, of course, must be taken into consideration since the predominance of any particular cause varies from country to country. Although there were causes common to all Latin America, the reaction against positivism in each country emerged from a complex national situation, rooted in cultural, political, and philosophical conditions that make it difficult to isolate specific factors. Thus it is best to speak of predominant influences.

The first general cause is the deception that Latin American intellectuals experienced when reality did not measure up to positivism's promises and aspirations. Immediate and assured results were promised and anxiously awaited, but progress was slow and uncertain. To uphold the general principles and criteria that should be used in the study of social problems is one thing, but it is quite a different matter to develop a specific form of knowing in which an effective scientific procedure is applied in order to solve the concrete problems of a country.

Stark reality shattered many illusions. It soon became evident that divesting oneself of traditional prejudices was not sufficient. The ideal of a scientific knowledge of social reality, which had been converted into an idol, began to crumble in the face of difficulties, and the initial, naive optimism gave way to corroding pessimism.

Comte himself did not satisfy the expectations he had awakened and, to make matters worse, no thinkers who measured up to his standards emerged in Latin America. The majority were content to repeat the ideas of the master without being able to apply them to the reality in which they lived. Philosophical theory cannot be converted into dogma; rather, it needs a continuing creative direction since its application to reality is not a routine, mechanical task. The complexity of the reality surpasses theoretical schemes.

Another general reason is the deterioration Comte's positivism suffered in his own country. With no outstanding disciples, since Littre and Laffite were not capable of building on the ideas of their master, positivism began to lose its nerve when Comte died in 1857. In time, new critical ideas, such as those of Boutroux and Bergson, appeared in France and eventually they were used to support Latin American revolt.

One of the issues about which the dissatisfaction was most profound was liberty. Opposition of different kinds united around this issue to repudiate positivism's empirical stance. Some of the opposition was philosophically bent, some was political, and some was aesthetically oriented.

The indiscriminate application of the principle of causality to every existing thing led positivism to deny freedom to man. Psychology was a biological science and the supposed freedom of choice or creation was felled by a scientific guillotine. The Argentine José Ingenieros carried this point of positivist doctrine to an extreme.

Theoretical objections to determinism acquire a great momentum in the moral realm. No one can be responsible for an act if it is determined, the critics of positivism claimed, influenced perhaps by their reading of Kant. Fires, hurricanes, and epidemics are not responsible for the deaths they cause. But men are indeed responsible because they have free choice; they are masters of their conduct and thus deserve punishment or praise. If the conduct of men were determined by causes or factors alien to their will, they would deserve neither praise nor punishment. Furthermore, suffering, disciplined effort, the struggle against sin, and other noble actions would lose their meaning. It was natural for the works of Henri Bergson to be received with great enthusiasm in Spanish America, on the basis of his refutation of determinism and his defense of liberty.

Another reason for the Latin American rejection of determinism was the implicit denial of aesthetic creation. Because they are gifted with a great aesthetic sensitivity and creative capacity, as is evident in the work of Rubén Darío and many other writers and artists, Latin Americans could not accept a mechanical explanation of the creative process. And many refuted positivism because it denied or was unable to explain creation in art, as is the case with Deústua.

However, the principal reason for the rejection of positivism with respect to freedom came from the political realm. In some instances, as in Mexico, positivism was associated with a dictatorship that had been overthrown; in others, Cuba, for example, it supported the colonial status quo over against the possibility of independence to which many aspired. In all the countries, suffering, first under Spanish oppression and then under a succession of dictators, had been too extensive for anyone to be ready to set freedom aside. Indeed, freedom had become the battle flag. If positivism did not make room for freedom, then positivism must be abandoned.

Alejandro Korn succinctly expresses the state of mind of the men of that time when he writes, "We cannot accept a philosophy which obliterates human personality, reduces its unity to a biological phenomenon, denies it a right to forge its own values and ideals and prohibits thought from transcending the limits of empirical existence."[1]

In addition to the reasons discussed above, a theoretical reason also influenced tendencies to reject positivism. The distinction, developed by Windelband, Dilthey, Rickert, and others, between the sciences of nature and those of the spirit became significant and influential and opened up the possibility of limiting positivism to its own forte, i.e., the physical and biological realm. In time, a new approach to the study of human problems emerged, which emphasized value, purpose, novelty, and creation over the natural realm. Thus, reality was divided in two and each part corresponded to a special type of knowledge. The establishment of these forms of knowledge, that of the subjective spirit and of the objective spirit or culture, was a major concern of the generation following the positivists, and the distinction between these two types of science persists even yet. Sciences of the spirit (*Geisteswissenschaften*) were thus separated from positivist domination and began to develop independently.

The dissatisfaction in Latin America and the ideas coming from Europe hastened the search for new approaches. In this search, appeal was made to political aspirations as well as to aesthetic and religious experience, although the spirit of religiosity, perhaps, played a more important role than religion. Metaphysical preoccupation, suppressed by positivism, experienced a rebirth. General dissatisfaction was encouraged by philosophers such as Boutroux, Bergson, and Croce, who had overcome positivism in Europe and were traveling new paths.

In each country, the reaction against positivism took on a characteristic expression, although the dissatisfaction itself was fairly uniform throughout Latin America. Mexico, however, gave first expression to the dissatisfaction and shaped it into a unique series of events. With the fall of the dictatorship of Porfirio Díaz in 1911, positivism also fell, for its foundations already had been undermined.

In 1909, a group of young men who later acquired well-deserved renown in the field of philosophy and letters founded the "Ateneo de la Juventud" (Atheneum of Youth). They studied the classics, especially Plato and Kant, and contemporary philosophers who had rejected positivism, such as Bergson and Croce. The influence of Nietzsche and Schopenhauer, who had thrown their weight against the narrow scientistic emphasis of positivism, was also felt. Following these studies lectures were given in which positivist doctrine was roundly criticized and new ideas were proposed. Of that group two men are especially well known as philosophers, Antonio Caso and José Vasconcelos. Selections from their writings are included in this book.

In Argentina the struggle against positivism was quite different. In the first place, positivism was not involved in any political movements. Furthermore, positivism had had an effective role in the development of educational institutions and, through José Ingenieros, had acquired renown in scientific and philosophical circles.

The two most distinguished figures in the struggle against positivism in Argentina were Alejandro Korn and Coriolano Alberini. Perhaps the latter, although less gifted in creative ability, had more influence than the former in casting it out of official teaching programs. A caustic spirit, Alberini allowed no truce with positivism in the University of Buenos Aires, an institution of which he was dean of the faculty of philosophy and letters on several occasions. Korn was less aggressive and fought positivism through his own sound, original philosophical position. In addition to his writings, his major contribution was encouraging the formation of a group of students whose philosophical orientation was foreign to positivism. Francisco Romero, who was introduced to philosophy through reading Spencer, felt the influence of the group that surrounded Korn. Thus in Argentina, positivism was overcome through the development of a different philosophical orientation rather than through sharp polemics.

Similar reactions are found in other Latin American countries. Metaphysics, heatedly attacked by Comte, returned to the fold. In some cases, this was due to the renewal of the classical concerns of Christian philosophy, and in others, to the rise of philosophical speculation in contemporary German thought.

PHILOSOPHICAL THOUGHT AFTER POSITIVISM

In the aftermath of positivism, four stages have emerged in the development of philosophical thought. The first is referred to as the stage of the "founders." These were the men who first rejected positivist thought although, in some cases, they are also included in the ranks of the positivists, since this was the philosophical position they first espoused. The "founders" were Deústua in Peru, Caso and Vasconcelos in Mexico, Korn in Argentina, Vaz

Ferreira in Uruguay, and Farias Brito in Brazil. Dependent first on French philosophers such as Boutroux and Bergson, and later on German philosophers—Nietzsche, Husserl, Dilthey, Heidegger, Scheler, Hartmann, Jaspers—as well as the Italian Croce, the "founders" developed a new orientation in Latin American philosophy. They did not form a school nor did they propose to do so, but they did formulate new approaches and develop new attitudes and methods of work.

The generation following the "founders" continued their thrust, but it was free from the polemic with positivism that had influenced the formation of that founding generation. Francisco Romero is the major figure here, and he, together with Ramos and Astrada, is included in the present work. This generation is characterized by an intense interest in the problem of man and by the influence of historicism, phenomenology, and existentialism.

The third stage emerges with the work of those born around the year 1910. In this group, the influence of German thought continues to be predominant, in some cases because of studies in that country—García Maynez and Llambías de Acevedo, for example—and in others, because of the influence of exiled Spanish philosophers such as José Gaos and Joaquín Xirau.

The prominent figures in the second stage were men whose professional preparation was not in philosophy but in law, medicine, or military science. In this third stage, however, almost all have pursued university studies in philosophy. The development of the discipline becomes more professional and technical, although less dramatic, but it is also more responsible and specialized. None attempts to elaborate a complete philosophical system, such as that of Vasconcelos with its metaphysics, ethics, and aesthetics. Instead of great encompassing works, specialized monographs were the rule. Indeed, a certain sparseness stemming from self-critical attitudes characterized their publications. At the same time, there was an increase in the number of those who studied philosophy, and interest in the field became broader as new departments were established in the universities that lacked them, such as those in Tucumán and Córdoba in Argentina, the Central University in Venezuela, as well as universities in Colombia and Panama. This tendency has continued to the present. The list of thinkers who belong to this generation is very long. Four of them are represented here: Reale, Zea, Miró Quesada, and Frondizi.

The fourth generation is the most active. Those from the first and second generations whose works appear in this collection have died. Those from the third generation [except for Frondizi who died in 1983] continue their intellectual labor, which has been clearly defined in their published work. Many of those in the fourth generation, however, are still developing their philosophical perspective and their principal works have not yet appeared. Hence, only selections from two authors have heen included here: Augusto Salazar Bondy and Arturo Roig.

At this point, the perspective becomes more complex due to the increasing number of persons who seriously pursue philosophical studies and the greater diversification in interests and currents of thought. To be sure, the traditional interest in German philosophy has remained; however, contemporary British and American influences, such as those of Alfred North Whitehead, Bertrand Russell, C. I. Lewis, R. B. Perry, and John Dewey, have had an increasingly significant impact since Frondizi began to introduce them after he returned in 1936 from his studies at Harvard. In more recent years, attention has been focused on logical positivism and analytic philosophy. Examples of this interest are the journal *Crítica,* published in Mexico, and the Argentine Society for Philosophical Analysis. Serious studies in the philosophy of science began under the contagious enthusiasm of Mario Bunge and continued with other scientists committed to philosophical study. This period also reflects a resurgent interest in Marxism, although no single person is outstanding as a leader of the group. The most significant influences of this period are Jean-Paul Sartre, in his existentialist as well as Marxist periods, Merleau-Ponty, and the analytical school.

These four stages overlap in many cases because they do not reflect movements but individuals who respond to their own interests. A man such as Deústua, who lived to be ninety-six years old, developed beyond his positivist orientations and made significant contributions in both the first and second stages. The work of others, such as Romero and Astrada, permits them to function in different stages also. Some of the philosophers, with the passage of time, changed and developed their views, as in the case of Astrada, who turned from existentialism, as found in Heidegger, to Marxism and thus is included in a more contemporary group.

It would be vain indeed to summarize the thought of those mentioned above. And, in any case, the more important figures in this book speak through selections from their own works, with each selection preceded by a brief introduction to aid in understanding the text.

Rather than summarize philosophical views, we would prefer to delineate the principal characteristics of Latin American philosophy of this century taken as a whole, recognizing, of course, that all of these characteristics cannot be applied in the same sense to each of the philosophers.

The first characteristic focuses on the background of the men under consideration. Most of them engaged in extensive studies in the humanities and even those who had formal training in biology are well grounded in literature, as reflected in their poetry and in their knowledge of contemporary and classical literary works, as is the case of Korn. This humanistic background proves to be an asset as well as a liability. The asset is the breadth of interest and the liability is a lack of empirical grounding, logical rigor, and conceptual and terminological precision. Generally, Latin American philosophers are competent writers. Korn, Caso, and Romero are good examples. At least they are concerned with the form of their expression,[2] a concern that occurs only exceptionally in North American philosophers. Along these lines, Latin Americans have followed the tradition of continental Europe, and in more recent times, that of Spain, with special reference to Unamuno and Ortega.

The second characteristic is a concern for social and political problems. Philosophy is not pursued as a disinterested form of knowledge, but as an orienting guide for individual and social conduct. Thus, its study is not neutral but passionate, because different philosophical views lead to different life styles. Man and his proper destiny are the issues to be decided and it is difficult to remain objective when the meaning of life is at stake. The excessive passion and polemic characteristic of Latin American philosophy is not due, as some would believe, to an overindulgence in emotion but to the type of problem with which it is concerned. The North American philosopher maintains his serenity because he studies technical problems, focusing on methodology and semantics where there is no significant play of emotions. Furthermore, the solutions to these issues do not significantly affect one's way of life, as is also the case in scientific fields. In Latin America, however, there are true conversions that change the personality of the philosopher when he alters his position with respect to the fundamental problems of life.

The concern for ethics, politics, and social philosophy explains the commitment the Latin American philosopher experiences. He does not seek to interpret reality through the mere desire to know; rather he is in search of a mode of conduct for himself and his fellow man. Thus, he becomes committed to a style of life for his country and the theory leads to action that often, unfortunately, weakens the theory and may reduce it to propaganda.

Theoretical aspects are of less concern than the practical consequences the theory may have, especially with respect to political, social, and educational reform. This tendency, present in many philosophical orientations, acquires a high degree of intensity in the case of positivism and Marxism. It is true that in more recent times philosophy has been pursued for its theoretical value, but it is no less true that the major concern has been with issues in human conduct.

The concern for the problems of national life and the commitment the Latin American philosopher makes explain the popularity that philosophy has in Latin America, in contrast to the esoteric attitude in the United States. The leading newspapers in Buenos Aires, Mexico City, Caracas, and other capitals frequently publish philosophical articles, and works in philosophy are sold in large quantities.

The interest of the philosopher as a philosopher in political problems has its counterpart in the interest of the politicians in philosophy. Eduardo Frei, who was a politician since his youth and the president of Chile from 1964 to

1970, was an eloquent example of this concern. In 1940 he published a book entitled *Politics and the Spirit*, in which he stated the philosophical justification of his political activities. The work lacks an original theoretical quality as it is based on the thought of someone else, namely, Jacques Maritain. It is important, however, that a politician should feel the need for developing a philosophical justification of his work. In his judgment, politics is an activity that proposes a style of life that finds its roots in philosophy. The same occurs with a former president of Chile, Salvador Allende, who, likewise, was concerned with the philosophical foundations of his social reform although his perspective was Marxist and, thus, different from that of Frei. This is a significant contrast to what happens in the United States. Here, politics as well as business are activities unrelated to philosophy. In all probability, neither Truman, Eisenhower, Johnson, Nixon, nor Reagan has given as much as an hour to searching for the philosophical foundations of his political activity or of his actions as president. To understand the significance of Latin American philosophy one must recognize the intimate link with the problems of the sociocultural milieu. Such a task is not isolated from reality, but it is the formulation of a theory in support of a praxis. Thus one can understand why people should become emotionally involved in the support of one view rather than another, since they lead to quite different modes of behavior.

With the exception of the traditional forms of neo-Thomism, Marxism, and to some degree neo-Kantianism and Mexican existentialism (Hyperion Group), one cannot speak of philosophical schools in Latin America. One is confronted rather with thinkers difficult to classify within the usual categories. Furthermore, they do not form schools and their students adhere more to a moral attitude than to the ideas of the teachers.

It is interesting that in Latin America, which is predominantly Catholic, there have been few thinkers of the first rank within that tradition. Those of a Christian orientation, Alberto Rougés and Antonio Caso, for example, do not fit into the traditional molds. Perhaps an explanation is to be found in that for Latin Americans, Thomism is not a strictly philosophical position; rather it is weighted with confessional and political purposes. Thus, new possibilities within that tradition are not explored. What is sought, rather, are arguments to defend a previously adopted position. Thus, the predominant writings in this tradition tend to attack or defend rather than pursue a theoretical investigation free from prejudice.

With a few exceptional cases, much the same is true of Marxism. Although it is the political philosophy that is more widespread, there are no exceptionally capable Marxist philosophers. For Latin American Marxists, doctrine is something that must be studied, proclaimed, and defended; critical investigation is a matter of secondary importance. In Thomism as well as in Marxism the proselytizing emphasis takes precedence over theoretical quality.

Neither Saint Thomas nor Marx, to be sure, would adopt such an attitude were they to appear on the scene. They would not reiterate philosophical positions with a lack of critical spirit and creative ability, as their followers do. Rather, they would elaborate a new theory, taking into consideration the significant historical events and scientific discoveries that have occurred since their deaths.

These two positions are the exaggeration of a characteristic that is frequent in Latin American thought. Theory is often converted into a dogma upon reaching these shores. When confronted by a theory one is forced to take sides and either defend or attack it. Thus, in philosophical writings, an affirming and often dogmatic attitude prevails, an attitude not concerned with giving reasons but one seeking to defend a position. One speaks of "being loyal" to the adopted doctrine. There is a lack, therefore, of a critical spirit, a creative capacity, and a desire to search. It would seem Latin Americans have inherited this dogmatic attitude from the Spaniards among whom one affirms one's personality by making shocking statements without regard for the facts. Good reasons and empirical evidence are of less importance than the assertive tone and the degree of intense personal conviction.

At present, Latin American philosophy is in a stage of normality. Philosophy is taught in most secondary schools and in the principal universities, and most of these institutions have centers for philosophical research. There is also significant interest in the history of philosophy as well as in systematic thought: specialized journals and reviews are published, national and international congresses are held on a regular basis, excellent translations, with scholarly commentaries, of classical as well as contemporary authors are published, as are original works of international significance. It should be understood however that the quality of philosophical studies is not the same in all countries. As outstanding examples one might point to Mexico and Argentina. Generally speaking, Central American countries, with the exception of Costa Rica, are those with the lowest level. In all, however, significant progress is evident, not primarily in the number of original thinkers, but because philosophical activity is found in many more institutions and receives broader support, and it has established roots in the culture and conscience of each nation. Since the "heroic" stage in which philosophy existed during the latter part of the last century and the early part of the present century has been definitely surpassed, one can hope that the best fruits will be those of the future.

R. F.

NOTES

1. Alejandro Korn, *Obras* (La Plata: Universidad Nacional de La Plata, 1938), 3:279–80.
2. This characteristic, together with their political awareness and pedagogical leanings, was pointed out by José Gaos in three articles. (See Bibliography.) These contain perceptive observations, but unfortunately they are not examples of good literature or clarity of expression.

Part One

Man